# Your Mind is God's Point in You

Hemf Kognov

2

# DO  YOU WANT

# TO  HELP  YOURSELF ?

## HEMF  KOGNOV

Order this book online at www.trafford.com
or email orders@trafford.com

Most Trafford titles are also available at major online book retailers.

Printed in the United States of America.

ISBN: 978-1-4669-4114-4 (sc)
ISBN: 978-1-4669-4113-7 (e)

*Trafford rev. 06/06/2012*

 www.trafford.com

North America & international
toll-free: 1 888 232 4444 (USA & Canada)
phone: 250 383 6864 ♦ fax: 812 355 4082

I dedicate this book to
whole my relatives.
And to individuals, who
touched my life.

# Contents:

Foreword                                              11

1. I aspire to find  God.                             17

2. Please help yourself to be happy.        49

3. Praying.                                           57

4. I send my love feelings into the Sky  74

5. About  Israel.                                   115

6. "LIFE  AND  AFTERLIFE."              121

# FOREWORD.

Dear human beings! You can help
yourself. You could help others.
-How?
Be your Best. Do your Best.
Wish others the Best, or don't think
about them.
Even a child can be his Best. Yes!
A child can act Best, can talk Best.

It is wise to educate your kids in life's
values, in social studies, in historical
happenings. Also teach your kids
to talk, to communicate, to listen.

About man's and woman's health.

It helps to hope for the best, to Think the best Thoughts for yourself, about yourself. Positive Thinking is good medicine. Every today find for what to thank yourself, to love yourself.

Give yourself  time to Think.
When your Mind reminds you about something, thank Him. Every today love your Mind more and more.
Mental  health is very important for us.

Man have problems with their heart.

A man at 38 died of a heart attack.
-Why?  He was a lucky person.
He owns a business. But he was angry
at his family, at other people, angry
at many things, happenings.

Why do women develop cancer?
Women worry about many things.
They  BELIEVE  that they can become
sick.  Women blame themselves much.

To have a healthy heart, to be healthy or
healthier, be glad to be yourself.

Like having whatever you have.

Fill okay or feel fine by doing any job
you have to do.  Or find different work.

Be not willing to have more, more, more
if it is not necessary for you to have.

Please always hope for the best,
do not  HOPE  for the worst.

Be careful, don't invite the devil.
Devil appears in many faces.

A pretty thing in one building.  But
it tells: "In memory of our neighbor."
Too many people in that building

became sick.  Too many people starve.

Be sincere in good Thinking and don't
have any doubts.  Or your positive
thinking would not happen.

Dear  Reader,  I wish you everyday
to be in peace with yourself.
Please let yourself every today
to feel at easy.

Know every today that it would
happen to you, what you think can
happen, what you prefer to happen.

I ASPIRED TO FIND GOD.

I was born in Moscow, USSR.
My family works and lives on a farm.
This farm is located in Moscow's city
Kunzevo. My Mother milks cows
and does some bookkeeping.
The Father cares for horses.

I was 3-years-old when my family was
accused of Zionism, and banished out
from Moscow to Muslim Uzbekistan.

Mother and I were sent out by a
goods-train. It took us 2 month

till we came to far south Uzbekistan.

My Father had to walk on foot.
He came 6 month later than we
arrived.  His legs were swollen.

My Mother was bathing and healing
the Father's legs.  A neighbor visited
us and fell in love with my Mother.

The neighbor went to KGB and told
them bad things about my Father.
1937 at night 2:30 am a witness and
2 KGB officers came in to our house.
They searched all over.

I was awaked, out from the little bed
on my Father hands, with my head
on Father's shoulder.

KGB officers found nothing, but they
take away my dear Father.

Tribunal court put my 31-year-old
Father in jail. There he was abused.

My dear Father died at age 35. My
Father Israel is always young to me.

In the era of Khrushchev my innocent
Father was justified. I was hoping to

return to Moscow. I applied for a
permit to live in Moscow, but was
not allowed to do so.

Whole my life I want, I long to live
in Moscow. That was my birthplace.

It is the capital city, a beautiful one.
I love this city. For my Mother and
for me, for my own family no
permit to live in Moscow.

Russian Bolshevik Revolution 1917
did blame for bad happenings, for
poor life the best people in Russia.

Spiritual leaders, other intellectual
people, and Wealthy people were
killed or murdered.

Millions more people were put in
prisons.  Churches, Mosques,
Synagogues were destroyed or
used for other purposes.

In regards to God the population
was told:  "Don't believe there
is a God.  It is a lie."

God was denied from everywhere.
People were afraid to talk about God,

to worship God.

I went to school. There I was taught
that uneducated, dark, poor, and old
people do believe in God. "You would
be educated. Know: There is no God.
We remove rivers. We grow new
fruits, vegetables. We fly high in the
Sky. No one is above."

I finished two colleges. I worked as
a teacher for 28 years.

I raised 2 kids and was in doubt
if God exist.

In Holocaust my Jewish relatives
in Ukraine were murdered and killed.
Witnesses of Holocaust asked:
  "Where is God?"

My Grandmother Minzya was at
that time with me in Uzbekistan.
My Grandmother believed there is
a God.  Her Father studied the Torah,
and told her much about God.
Believing in God helped my
Grandmother in hard life situations.

In year 1979 my family and  I
immigrated to the USA, Minnesota.

There were Spirit institutions. I was
confused and begin to search for
evidence if there is a God.

I attended lectures and worship.
I read a lot. I found religious books,
studied philosophy books, got
psychology and medicine books.

This education and many happenings

in my life gave me some evidence
about God's existence.

In MN my Husband's death occurred .

After a while my mother became sick.

My Mother can't get out of bed for
over three years.  I care for her.
Then my dear Mother passed away.

All of that and my own life tell
me more about God's presence.

Several years I was dealing with leg
cramps.  I consulted with doctors.
I got some advises.  I exercised, so on.

In year 1997  I awoke from a major
cramp in my left leg from bottom

to the knee.  I try to get out of bed
and my right leg begins to cramp.
All I can, I did.  Nothing helped me.
The pain in both legs was unbearable.

I could not suffer any more that pain.
I sat on a chair.
I beg God to help me.
In 2 minutes whole cramping stopped!

It was my first request to God for help.
That was my evidence:
Great God is real.

I start asking myself questions.

How did God know what is
going on with me?
Wasn't God busy doing
something else?

Who stopped my painful cramps?
That answer appeared in my head

   -I stopped your cramps.
I am your God. I was blown up
in you with your first breath. I'll be
with you as long, as you are alive

   -How to believe this?
My legs start shaking. They shake so

hard, that I must hold on to the chair.

My whole body tightens up.
I don't know what is going on.
It is not morning yet.

All my Thinking was: "Hold on to
the chair. Don't fall down."
This shaking goes on a few minutes.
Then my legs stop to shake.

-Do you believe now that
   I am your God?
-How should I call You?
-You can call Me: God. Mind.

God's Points.  Soul.  Spirit.

Surprise: God answers my questions
-Yes, everyone's God can answer
  your personal questions.

-Where do You locate in me?
-I can locate everywhere in you.
  Usually I locate in your
  head and in the neck-back brain.

-As God above you, I am an Air-Force.

Your God includes 3 God's Points.
Every person's structure is like yours.

One God's Point locates in you.
Second God's Point can be above
you, around you.  Your third
God's Point is in the Sky.

I, God's Point in you, feel the same
what you feel.  Everything in you
performs now, feels right now.

I imply your thinking in
your body's function.

I help you to do
what you are willing to do.

To be with Me: You have to talk to
Me.  Or think-whisper.  You can
write to Me. You may ask questions.

When you have a friend, relative,
a child - you are talking to them.
I, your God's Point, am closer
to you than any relative.

A picture shows up in my head.
Working as a teacher, I have to
write much.  My wrist curves,
when I was a child.

My right hand became tired.

I beg the air above me for a little
vacation to my painful hand.

It takes some time. Once at wintertime
it was slippery.  I fell down and the
right hand was broken at the wrist.
I have the vacation for my dear hand.

I did not think about such a vacation.
I stopped writing for 2 month.


My Dear God or my Dear God's Points
answer questions   ONLY   IF   I   ASK

Dear Reader! Who you are, where
you live, any language you speak,
any faith you belong:

You experience your human life.
You yourself know how your life
was. Maybe you are remembering
what already happened to you.

I remember what happened to me.
I experience my life.
My life was full of losses, troubles,
fear, sicknesses, and addictions.
I also become depressed, forgetful.
I was abused.

A few years ago I retired.
50 years I worked already.

Ramadan fasting now I experience about
3 month in 1 year.  I often eat once at
evening time.  But I drink much water.
Boiling water, something sweet is my tea.

I follow Jewish fasting.  Thanks
to God, I am normally healthy.
I live one day at one time.
I appreciate having whatever I have.
I like to do, what I have to do.

If I don't need or don't like something,

I give it away or I let it go out.

This book tells about me, about my
life, and how I helped myself.
That book tells how you
can help yourself.

I share with you my experience,
knowledge, and logic information
about: God. Life. Health. Love.
Everyone can become healthy or
healthier, happy or happier.

We can do better now.  We can be better
right now.   Today is a New Day.

Good morning to you.

And please be easy on yourself.
Who likes to know if Dear
God's Point exists in you?

You can prove that God is with you.
-How?

Ask YOURSELF the Safest Question.
The Safest Question is:

" What Is Best For Me
   To Do Now ?"

Every human being may ask the Safest
Question whenever you need God's help

STOP. Yes, stop doing whatever you do.
Then ask the Safest Question. Your God
or your Dear God's Points know what
is going on with you.

Ask that question about one thing
at one time.  You can solve one
problem at one time.

To ask the Safest Question,
You need to be in a quite place or
plug your ears.  Close your eyes.

Ask the Safest Question slowly.
Then relax hoping that you'll get a
prudent advice. In a few minutes
a thought would arrive in your head.

Whenever You ask that question,
wait for an answer.
Understand the answer.
If you need, ask your question again.

It is evening time. I try to lock my
main door for the coming night.
The lock does not work well.
I'm the only one in that apartment.

Danger thoughts came in to me.
I asked myself the Safest Question.

-Lock your door, as best as it can
  lock.  Hope that You'll be safe.

God's miracle is:  We can change our
Thinking.  Then our feelings change.

 We may change our Thoughts
 about everyone, about everything.

We, people, make mistakes.  We must
learn from our own mistakes.  Please
forgive yourself.  Forgive other people

Don't blame yourself.
Do not blame anyone.

Best for you not to cheat on yourself.
Your own conscience is your judge.

In Young America's June 2003
calendar, President Reagan tells:
"The government's view of the
  economy can be summed up in
  a few short phrases.

If it moves, tax it.  If it keeps
moving, regulate it.  If it stops
moving, subsidize it."

But President Reagan lowered taxes.
He lies to himself.  His feelings are hurt
Ronald Reagan punished himself.
President Reagan become sick.
He was sick for many years.

In your human life it is best to be honest
with yourself, with your feelings.

Otherwise you punish yourself,
relatives, or your loved ones.
A governor punished his committee,
his business, his country.

God's advice is:  "Talk to Me or

think-whisper. You can write to Me."

I locked all my keys in the car.
It takes much time to open the car.
Now I am talking: "The car is off.
The keys are with me. Good-bye
my lovely car. And thanks."

Talking takes time. I slow. But it
is less time than to open my car.

I hit my elbow at the refrigerator. At
once I talk: "Please and thanks. Best.
Thanks. Please help my elbow to heal"
I pray that 3 times.

Then: "My Dear God's Points,
I love You. Yes. Yes. Yes."

In many other occurrences my Dear
God's Points are helping me.

Using the word 'Please' I beg
my Dear God or my Dear God's
Points to help me or to heal me.

My Dear God I beg to help me today
to deal with my body's temperature,
to see better, to hear better, to ease
my cough, to fall asleep faster, to be
alert. When I need an advice. So on.

Before I go to bed I love, I thank
my Dear God for His today's help.

Even if my vision is little better,
I'm thanking my Dear God for
helping me today to see better.

My Dear God's Points today I love.
I thank them for Their helping.

While I'm working at that book,
I have to think that way.  To pick up
a plate, I whisper 'Best and thanks.'
Same whispering when I do anything
else, dressing up, undress, so on.

44

A long time ago about healing,
I found in a doctor's book an advice.

"If you hurt yourself, take 3 deep
breath in and out. At that time think
about your pain, your burn, so on.
Then let yourself to heal.

For 10-15 minutes free your Mind
of that thinking. Start thinking
about something else.
In that 10-15 minutes your Mind
is healing whatever happens to you."

I love  Dearest  Almighty  God.

I love my  Dear  God.
I love my  Dear  God's  Points.

Everyone needs love. Something
good we can find in every person.

I was working at first shift.  From
the bus I walk while it is dark.
A black man comes across. He is upset

-Dear, I'm glad to meet you.
You are so young, so healthy.
Can you guide me 2 blocks north?

We walk together.  "Thank you much.

It is very nice of you. I wish you
all the best, dear person."
Now the young man is smiling.

It is okay to love human beings.
You may love as many people
as you prefer. Your love can be
more or less saturated.

For the freedom of our Press I'm
thanking Dearest Almighty God every
morning, when my newspaper is in.

For the Liberty in USA I really love
and praise Dearest Almighty God.

## PLEASE HELP YOURSELF
## TO BE HAPPY

Human beings do long for happiness.
You can help yourself to feel happy.

Whole daylong you were doing
something to better the life on Earth.
Now do something good for yourself:
List up all your Today's activity.

Your Mind is involved in all your
doings.  Please thank your Mind.

For me it works that way.

1. During the day or at evening-time
I list everything I did today.
If something needs to be
finished, I make a note.

2. I went over the listing again.
Now I am thinking about every
item on my list. I know what
each thing means for me.
I know how I accomplished it.

| Morning time. | Evening time. |
|---|---|
| 1. Checks book! | 1. Mail. |
| 2. Garbage. | (2) A letter. |
| 3. Henry. | 3. Shopping. |

| | |
|---|---|
| 4. Breakfast. | 4. The stove! |
| 5. Post office. | (5) Healing. |
| 6. Gas station! | 6. Trifles. |
| (7)Going to work. | 7. TV news. |

At the list 'Checks book' monthly
bills are paid. One deposit was made.
A few pages at the checkbook were
balanced. I love my Mind for that.

My 'trifles' include: To make the bed.
To dress up, undress. Hair. The toilet.
To drink my everyday water. To wash
my hands, so on. Usually I soap my
hands 3-4 times at one wash hand.

Very important items, I circle,
or I put a mark!

I'm writing the listing for
myself every Today.
Listing helps me to be happy.
It is a joy-therapy for me.
It would bring joy to you.

We are, what   we are.
You may help yourself.

Please be glad to be You.
Your feelings would be up.
Tell yourself: "I did all that!

I drive. I worked. I made my listing.
I eat, drink, and sleep! Today my
energy was fine!" And tell so on.

To sharpen my memory, I'm using
a calendar. Yesterday was Monday.
On Tuesday I write in Monday's place
what I remember about Monday.

I know how my health was yesterday.
First line in my calendar is:
'I praise You my Dear God.'
Going trough yesterday's calendar
 I love my Dear God very much.
 I love my Dear God's Points also.

I thank yesterday and welcome today.
Usually I'm doing the calendar
in early morning time.

For myself I'm writing an everyday
diary on two sides typing pages.

The diary is about what goes on
in my Today's life.  Every today
has it's own date.  Everyday has
it's own weight.

A few sentences I write up every day.
Many days I'm writing much.
It was many titles in my dairy.

Now the title is:

"My Dear God and my Dear God's
  Points, today  I  Love  You."   or

 "My Dear God and my Dear God's
  Points, today I love  You.  Yes." or

 "My Dear God and my Dear God's
  Points, today I love  You.  Yes!"

It differs how long my love is lasting
when I pronounce that sentence.

It matters how I'm feeling right now.

## PRAYING

How I pray and about what I pray.
For Dearest Almighty God and for my
Dear God I'm praying at a window.
The Sky is above me.

Giving many thanks and sending
my love really helps me.
Every today I pray in that order.

After my awake, sitting on the
bed's edge I pray: "My Dear God and
my Dear God's Points, thank You for
the night. Tonight I slept about fine.

Good morning.  Lets have a normal
day.  Please be easy on Yourself.

I hope: To be healthy today.
To do best whatever I do.
And to feel good."

My head nodded.  "Thank  You
very much my Dear God that it is
fine with You.  I really love You. Yes!"

Not every night I sleep the same.

My head also nods, if my Dear
God's Points agree with me.

When daylights start, I'm praying:

"Dearest Almighty God thanks a lot,
a lot, a lot  1.  For sending us today's
New Day.  Yes, yes, yes.  2.  Thanks
a lot, a lot, a lot that today I want to
care for myself, for my health.
Thanks. Yes, yes, yes.  3.  Thanks
a lot, a lot, a lot that I hope today for
the best.  Thanks. Yes, yes, yes.
Dearest  Almighty God, today
I love You, love You, love You."  or

Dearest  Almighty God, today I love
You, love You, love You. Yes!  or

Dearest Almighty God, today I love
You, love You, love You. Yes! Yes! Yes!

I continue to pray
"My Dear God, thank You very much
for being God's Point in me. Thanks.
Thank You very, very much for being
God's Points above me. Thanks.

Then: My Dear God
Today I love You 1. For helping me
to sleep 6 hours tonight. Thanks.
2. For things that are done. Thanks.
3. For my mind's work. Thanks.
4. For my today's healing. Thanks.

5. For being at my reach.  Thanks.
   Again and again I beg You: today
   please be Close to me.  Thanks.
   My  Dear God, I really need You
   and I really love You. Yes, yes, yes!

   My Dear God's Points, I love You
   also. Please be With me today.
   Thanks.  I really need You too.
   Yes.  Yes.  Yes.

   I continue praying.
   My  Dear  God, I hope to be healthy
   today.  Thanks.  I hope to have the
   energy and mind (or: wisdom, spirit)

that I would need today.  Thanks.
I also hope to feel good about
my today, about myself.  Thanks.

Today I love  You, love  You,
love  You my Dear God
and my  Dear  God's  Points.

-My dear client, thank you for
  loving Me today.

-My Dear God, thank You much for
  Your respond.  Thank You very much
  for talking to me.  Thank You very,
  very, very much for being You."

When I tell 'Dearest Almighty God'
an Air- Force arises above my face.

When I tell 'My Dear God' a thinner
Air- Force is facing me or above me.

I'm  closing my eyes and
continue to pray at the window.

For what I love Dearest Almighty God

My Mind works normal.  I hope for
the best.  I wish everyone the best.
God's air helps me to heal.
My health is normal.  But I'm taking

a synthroid tablet. It is expensive now.

I have a home. A subsidies apartment
Thanks much for the program HUD.
My Social Security is small.
The country I left, pays me nothing.

It is winter time. The heating system
works in our senior building.
My kitchen has water that I use for
coking and drinking. The water is from
sources that Dearest Almighty God
creates for us, for me, for you.

Day's lights help me to see what

I have to see.  Everything is visible.
Air's oxygen helps me to breathe.
Over my head is a peaceful sky.
For the nature beauty, for the food.

Natural food does not have much sugar,
fats, potassium.  I wish the food would
become ripe on the ground it growth.
Food would taste so good, as  Dearest
Almighty  God  creates it to taste.

In my personal life I love Dearest
Almighty God every today.

At evening-time before I go to bed,

I pray at the window in that order:

"My Dear God, thanks for my today.
Two messages are prepared and sent
out. One person responds and we talk.
I'm very glad for my today's healing.
Some house work was done.
I worked at the computer today.

All of today's praying was about done.
Other days I thank for something else.

Today I love You, love You, love You
my Dear God, my Dear God's Points."

"Dearest Almighty God thanks a lot,
  a lot, a lot for sending us today's
  night time.  I need to rest.

For Israel's being safe today I love
You very much.  I wish the whole
world to remain in peace.

For my today's life thanks a lot.

Dearest Almighty God today I love You,
love You, love You. Yes. Yes. Yes!"

For Dearest Almighty God
I feel deepest love.

For my Dear God I feel
deep and very deep love.

For other people's Dear God
I feel deep and deeper love.

When I'm out of my home, I pray
outside.  An open place is okay.

I start praying with closed eyes
and plugged ears.

I tell  'Dearest Almighty God'  or
I tell  'My Dear God' and pray.

The apartment where I live.
At morning time I pray:

"My home, everything in it, and
everyone in my home:  That is me
and my Dear God's Points.  Today
I wish you all the best.  Please be
today your best.  Please and thanks."

I pray at evening time outside my door

"Our building, everything in it, staff,
residents, and me with my Dear God's
Points.  Today I wish you all the
best.  Please be your best for 24 hours.

Please and thanks."

I'm sending my thanks high into the Sky even if I'm not at a window.

For a home where I am in, I'm also praying. I'm thanking their family, their home, and wishing the family and the home all the best.

Dear Reader, if you would like, go to a window.

When nothing outside disturbs you, say: 'My Dear God.' Above your face

You'll see an Air- Force.

It's size is like a face, a head
or little larger.

You may start to pray.  It is up to you

A sunny spot in the air or near me
I'm seeing sometimes, or feeling.

It also happens.  I am disappointed
at some things, some happenings.

Often I ask my Dear God to help me
if in need.  Then I pray that praying:

"My Dear God.
Please help me today to feel normally best inside my body and outside my body. Thanks much. My Dear God, I really love You. Yes. Yes. Yes."

The same I pray when I went to bed. To be dressed up to go out. If I deal with my blanket. So on.

Many thanks for our Advantage Center. Thanks much to Volunteers.

Dear reader! Please find for what to thank, who to love. You'll feel better.

# I SEND MY LOVE
# FEELINGS INTO THE SKY

Let me put on some examples for what
I am thanking and sending my love
into the Sky at morning praying,
and at evening praying.


## A
1. Today my Mind is fine. I hope for
   the best.  I wish everyone the best.

2. For creating the needed energy in me.

3. For helping me to become at easy.

4. I talked to an aggressive authority.
   And we agree.  Thanks.

5. For teaching me to love. I found
   what was good in a stranger,
   who knocked today at my door.
   Everyone has something good in him.
  It is best to consider a person to be good

   Vatican Pope John Paul was a good
   person.  He loved all the people.
   He taught us to spread peace,
   friendship, and love.

Please be a good person. Then you'll
be able to feel good of being you.
You would be glad to be yourself.

All human beings can accept
these God's given values.

Please teach your child to become
a good person. He'll thank you.

-Can schools, games, books, TV,
music, and so on help us to teach
right things to our kids?

-It is for you, parents, to find out.

Usually children follow examples
that they see, hear, and play.

To spread any fear is wrong to do.
A dishonest person is peril.
Best is to teach kids good examples.

6. A few dishes are washed, dried,
and put on their place.

7. Today's laundry is done.

8. For a Democratic country is good to
forbid publishing hate and bad things.
Because that teaches people to do so.

9. For my ability today to pray.
   I really want to pray every today.


## B

1. For making me to look at the Sky
   at that moment.  I have seeing
   a beautiful Sky's picture.  The Sky
   shows us great paintings at Sunrise
   and at Sunset.  I try also to see
   the Sky once during the day time.

2. For the freedom of the press in US.
   Today's article has a sentence:

'At stake is our honor, our mobility, and our principles.'

Not many countries allow their press to write about all aspects in life.

3. For teaching me and helping me to act slowly, to talk slowly and politely. I'm acting now slowly, but I'm doing more in one day than I did before.

Positive thinking is good for you and good for me. It benefits our health.

4. For that lesson. An accident happened

A good Father and a teenage son were friends. They went hunting. The son is on a tree. His rifle is ready to fire. Tree's branch shakes. The bullet is in Father's neck. The Father was killed.

Dangerous is to have a gun in the house. It is your hidden enemy. Sooner or later the gun would fire.

5. For Your help to heal my today's emotions. My attitude matters for me

6. For teaching me to be willing to find out what is good in a person. When you

tell a person something good about him,
it awakes the best in a woman, in a man.

7. Today I cleaned the stove. I'm
   glad to do it.

8. It is a memorial day for my Mother.
   I light up a special lamp for my closest
   relatives. I love them. I think they are
   my angels now.

   Photos of my dead Mother, Father,
   Grandmother, and my Husband are
   upfront in frames. Every today I look
   at them and express my love to them.

For different reasons I love my Mother,
Father, Grandmother, and my Husband.

I also love my Grandfather, my other
Grandmother.  None of their  photos
I  have. They were killed in Holocaust.
I pray for my relatives every today.

That praying is included in my
morning praying.  Usually I pray at
early morning time.  If necessary,
I allow myself to perform the whole
praying to be done before noon time.

I'm very glad that I love all my alive

relatives and my in-laws.  When
I prefer, I pray for them.
My love flees different heights.

9. I worked on my spirit to be up.

My Dear God and my Dear God's
Points, I love You deeper and deeper


# C
1. For healing, healing, and healing
my  knee.  Now it is better.

I'm lucky to know about my God
and about my God's Points.

2. For Your advice how to make easier
   my today's life.  My everyday has
   it's own weights.

3. For helping me to solve this problem.
   At a given day I baby-sit my great-
   grandson for 8 hours once per week.
   I get a call to baby-sit him another
   day. But this other day I had to meet
   a situation in our building.
   How to be?  My dear God found
   a solution for me.

4. For my energy to do today's work.
   And for my hoping to do much.

5. For teaching me to Think about
   health and healing, if I hope to
   be healthy.  I should not Think
   Thoughts about sickness. Any Doubts
   don't let good Thoughts to happen.

6. For letting things to go out.
   Already I threw out much. And
   I'm still finding what to let go out.
   Today I also through out something.

7. Today's shopping was okay.  Now

I need to unpack.

8. For my today's listing.  It takes some
   time.  Thanks that it is already done.

9. Very fresh was the air today.
    It helps me  to cool off.
   God's weather is free.  God's lights
   are free.  God's water is free.
   God's Sky is free.  God's nature
   is free.  God's air is also free.

   It is fair that all elections do have
   free air, free broadcasting, free
   places, free press, and so on.

Dear People be responsible to vote,
when you are able to choose authorities
Please care about your country.  Yes.
Do care about the quality of life.

Thanks much to state MN for it's
voting process.  Ballots easily slide
into simple voting machines.  We
also have same day registration.


# D
1. For teaching me and helping me
   to talk with myself, for my thinking-

whispering.  I try to do it often.

2. For directing me where to find
   the lost ticket.  I'm happy about it.

3. About considering some people to
   be bad, do fingerprint and photo.

4. We give a good book to a relative.
   That book can help him, if he is
   willing to help himself.

5. For lifting up my head often. I hope
   that I'm seeing more and better.
   I think my back is straightening.

6. Today's vacuuming is done.
   It is work for me.

7. For teaching me to think about life,
   if I like to be alive.

   There  can be no arms in the whole
   world, if you human beings love one
   another.  Or don't think of others.
   Just do not hate anyone.

   Earth, water, sun, air, time, day lights,
   nature, so on are for everyone.  If you
   would be friendly to other people,
   they would not hurt you.  Their God

will know that you are a friend.

If you need sport activity, go and
do them. You don't need to fight
with one another.
Please compare results within
Yourself: How higher are you
jumping Today than Yesterday ?

8. A person can help himself (herself),
   if you are Willing to do so.

9. Thanks again to newspaper articles.

It is best for a country when population

is about identical wealthy.  Do you
know what happened in Russia
in 1917?  In Germany it happens.

Your wealth you could not take with,
when you go to heaven.  No one can.
Your love, your good deeds can
follow your Spirit.


### E
1. For helping me to clear my feelings.
   I called and left a message.

2. For today's advice to bend down and

up by doing my jobs, by dressing up, and undress. My joints are working thanks to God.

3. Today we found a neighbor's keys The neighbor was very thankful.

4. For giving me the energy to do, what I did already.

5. My little finger healed fully today.

6. For taking a nap. I lay down. My mind relaxed. It is easier for the blood to reach our brain.

7. For reminding me about my
   grandkid's wedding anniversary.

   My dear Grandmother Minzya was
   smart, educated in Jewish studies
   nice looking and a hard working girl.
   But she was poor.  She married
   a man, who was just a freighter.
   Lesbians and gays can also look down.

   "My younger daughter, do you really
      like that girl?  Fine.
      Let her be your closest friend.
   –Why?
      Because life must continue."

For kids matters their self-esteem.
Your child can be glad to be a boy
(a girl). Yes, kids should appreciate
themselves. Please help your kids
to love themselves.

8. For a lesson. To start an electro-lamp
   to turn away. Otherwise my eyes are
   hurt. Now sometime I close my eyes.

9. For helping me to divide a complete
   project into smaller parts. Then I don't
   worry myself about the whole project.

# F

1. For teaching me and helping me to
   slow. To do my best, I must slow.
   If I speed up, something bad happens:
   A car accident. I'm hurting myself.
   A statue was broken. Water spills out.

2. My daughter 'Agnes' drove home.
   Half mile away the car start to sound
   difficult. It went slower and slower.
   Thanks to Agnes' dear God that my
   daughter managed the situation.

3. For directing my looking where
   I should look. Today I did not pass

the first step at staircase.
I'm thanking for that much.

4. I fill on today 4 gallons kitchen
   water for my drinking and cooking.
   Thanks I have the energy to do it.

5. For teaching me and helping me to
   finish fully one project. Then only
   I start another project.

6. Dear people, please forbade yourself
   torture people, animals, anything.

7. A volunteer came in today and helped

me to work at the computer. I thank
that person every time, when he is in.
In USA many people are volunteering.

8. For sending us tonight. I long to go
   to bed. I hope to sleep well.
   Whole my life I didn't have enough
   time to sleep. I don't even pay
   attention to my dreams. I prefer
   to forget them. I did not discuss
   with anyone my dreams.

9. Today I nap and I worked much.
   My Dear God and my Dear God's
   Points I love You more and more.

# G

1. I baby-sit today my great-grandson
   3 year old 'Charles'. I love him.

2. For today's safe driving. I start to
   drive at age 48.

3. I hope to have the power to go
   through today, and to do what
   is necessary for me to do today.

4. For teaching me how to relax, and for
   helping me to relax. I'm not brave.
   I don't want to risk my life, my health.

5. An important thought I wrote up.
   It did not fly away.

6. Today I managed a few days' of
   incoming mail.  It is much junk in it.

7. For teaching me to talk to myself
   and helping me to do so.
   I'm a senior now.  It helps my
   Mind working normally fine.

8. I finished reading a Magazine.  I do
   appreciate getting written information

9. Today I'm glad to be myself.  Thanks.

# H

1. My Dear God, thanks much for all
   Your hints.  I wish, I notice most of
   them.  Your hints are very helpful.

2. For waking me up at that time.
   I need to make a call to another
   country, where time is different.

3. Today's newspaper tells about
   USA death penalties.

   As a teenager, I start to notice
   people's Thinking and my Thoughts.
   Deep Thoughts usually happen to us.

In 1993 Israel Prime Minister
Yitzhak Rabin and Palestine Authority
Yasser Arafat met on the White House
lawn. With president Bill Clinton's
help they are shaking hands.

Yitzhak Rabin pronounced:
'I was a soldier. I know what it
means to be in war. I am a soldier.
To create peace for Israel,
I like to die as a soldier.'
Someone had to kill him. He was
shot. He died as a soldier.

4. For teaching me what to read. I hope

that our Journalists tell us the truth.

5. You remind me about important dates.
   My friend's anniversary is coming up.

6. For a Newspaper Carrier yesterday
   I put out a gift and on a larger sheet of
   paper a thank you note. I'm surprised
   today: even the large sheet is out.

   For which reason the person takes with
   him that thank you note, he knows.

7. For Your, my Dear God, today's
   helping me.

8. For teaching me to not be afraid of
   myself.  My blanket's case is fighting
   with me.  It is on my neck, my chin,
   on my cheeks, at my nose, my hears.
   Again I'm asking the Safest Question.

   Unnecessary other things, happenings
   sometime bother me.

9. I enjoy looking on the Sky today.
   White clouds and spots fill on the Sky.
   Usually  it  happens  Friday  afternoon,
   Saturday and till noon at Sunday.  Also
   whites are in at Holidays.  Or the Sky
   is very light even on a rainy day.

In MN the weather is almost normal.
We have frost and snow even at the
beginning of November moth.  What
you think, I think, people think about
the climate can matter, does matter.

# I

1. I hope the computer and the
   printer would work today.

2. We worked much on our book.

3. For teaching me to be patient, to be
   willing to wait. To do it, is not so easy

4. For reminding me about Thoughts,
   things, happenings. Thanks

5. For Your advice: Let the answering
   machine handle unwanted phone calls

6. Today's 11-20-2005 Star Tribune
   about taxes: 'Lower effective
   state and local tax rates for
   seven-figure earners are unjustified.'

   For schools, roads, libraries, and so
   on the whole Country is responsible.
   The same about Nature, about all
   life's requirements.

The USA also appears to help some
world's Countries, happenings.
Where to get all needed money, if
not by taxing enough the richest?

Budget should balance always.  Do not
spend future generations' money.  They
would have to pay for their own expenses

7. I attended a Monthly Meeting already.
   It is still Daylight outside.

8. My Dear God thanks for answering my
   questing about debts. "A debit eats up
   your money.  Pay off your debts ASAP"

9. My Mind remembers what I did today.
   I prefer to have a clear Mind.
   By drinking alcohol, by using
   drugs, narcotics we abuse our Mind.

   My grandmother Minzya told me:

   "If you lose money, you lose nothing.
    If you lose your health, you lose half.
        If you lose your Mind,
        you lost everything."

   Now much is going on in life to confuse
   people's Minds.  Something occurs
   even to destroy the life on Earth.

Arms and everything else that are destroying people's life is devil.


## J

1. For inspiring the spirit in me.
   Even my energy is up.

2. Some house obligations are done.
   The mattress was rotated.

3. I ate my breakfast and hope
   to eat twice today.

4. Something else is also done.

Most of it is Mind work.

a. Working with our book I had to
   use the dictionary today.
b. Composed is a letter to my
   relative in Israel.
c. A donation was mailed out.
d. Morning praying is done.
   It is already 10 am.

My Dear God, and my Dear
God's Points, today I love You much.

5. I met a family. The husband became
   angry easily. Even a family needs love,

honesty, friendship, and discussions.

Then it would be less divorces, less
tragedies.  Love would prevail.

6. I'm reading a Ruby's Hanukah letter.
   He taught people to care for their
   own life.  Life can become better.
   The World would do better.

Please dear Reader, do care for yourself.
Love yourself, be easy on yourself. And
be willing to live as long, as possible.

7. I hope that people are able to

negotiate their problems.

We need to talk.  If we are willing to
Think deep, we can solve any problems

8. I think that people should properly
   care for planet Earth environment.
   Maybe then Nature would stop
   fighting with people.

9. I hope that my kids would have a safe
   flight.  The Sky is for everyone.


Dearest Almighty God is above us.

Dearest Almighty God
may I ask a question?

- Yes

- Why in the war and not only
  in a war people were
  tortured, killed, raped?

-You, human beings, have to teach
  kids and adults how to behave Best.

For people to be alive and not be
injured it must be no wars, no arms,
no fights in the whole world.

112

Human beings are able to Think,
to Speak, to Listen.

Mature people can and should
came to an Agreement.

Population and everyone of you
must Negotiate, to be fair.

Otherwise human's world
could be destroyed again.

- Dearest Almighty God thanks a lot
for Your answer. I love You very much

# ABOUT ISRAEL

For more then already 2 years I pray once
per day: "All human beings' Dear Gods
today I love You for letting yesterday
Jewish people in Israel civilians to stay
alive and not be injured.

For that I love You today all human
beings' Dear Gods.  Yes.  Today
I love You, love You,  love You.

I'm sending my love feelings high.

Dearest Almighty God.

Thanks a lot, a lot, a lot for that
praying.  It is helping for over 2 years.
So wonderful works love. Thanksss

For a few days I stopped praying
because in Israel some civil people
where not let to be alive.

Dearest Almighty God, thanks a lot,
a lot, a lot that now I can pray again
for all human beings' Dear Gods.

In year 2005 Rosh Hashanah and
Ramadan start the same day. Christmas
and Hanukah also start the same day.

Arabs, Christians, Jews and all other
nationals are God's kids.

At  Jewish  New Year I wish every
person on Earth:  Good health.
Wise thinking.  Much happiness.

Jews are a historic nation.
Jewish religion is a peaceful one.

Israel won the war when He was
attacked in year 1967.  It was a 6-day
war.  That is a Miracle victory.

There are over 20 Arab Countries

in the World.

Jewish people have only 1 Country for whole world's Jews.

Israel is not a large Country. Dearest Almighty God gave Israel to Jewish people.

Israel should not be divided.

Vice President Walter Mondale recalls  1978 peace accords.

"For political reason President

Jimmy Carter pushed Israel
 to give away Sinai."

"A failure of the Camp David
 process was it's lack of acceptance
 by significant parts of the Arab
 and Israel populations."


I really beg every human being
to be honest and to wish Israel
accomplish a  Just Peace Agreement.

## "LIFE AND AFTERLIFE."

Life is My, GOD'S, greatest gift for you, people. It is meant to bring Me happiness and joy. I, God, am doing all the best for you, people.

Life has to continue. Every man and woman should give birth to a child. For a couple it is best to have 2 kids.

No more than 3 kids. It is much work to raise good your child. The husband is responsible for wife's pregnancy. For a man it is easy to protect himself.

Who did not produce a child feels
lonely, jealous, disturbing after their
death. They suffer. I feel it.

I, GOD, must let them choose
to be anyone of an animal.

Bad people after their death
become birds.

Very bad people after their death
become reptiles.

Who commit suicide, terrorists
after their death become insects.

Animals, birds, reptiles, insects
possess only the Mind.

I, GOD, am connected with
Minds-Souls.  About political,
religion, other policies.
Don't correct a person's Mind.

People's death is My, God's, business.
No one else should kill anyone.

About your time to die, I would let
your God's Points to know.

If a family could not have kids,

they should adopt a child or two.

Normal parents and grandparents live usually three-four generations on Earth. From three to six generations more they are here, in the Sky with Me.

Then these people become alive again and again. They were born as new babies. They don't remember anything from their previous life.

Good people are thoughtful, honest, responsible, and thankful. They like to do their best, to be their best.

Right now you man and woman,
are Human beings.

I, ALMIGHTY GOD,
wish whole humanity: Health. Peace.
Friendship. Happiness. And Love.

Doing good and well your work is best.
Every person should find work to do it.
The work should not be too heavy,
too dangerous. It has to be enough
workers in a staff. Every worker
should be paid accordingly.

This message I received from Above.